This book belongs to

_____

COPYRIGHT © 1999, 2001 Nanci Bell
Gander Publishing
P.O. Box 780
Avila Beach, CA 93424
805-541-5523 • 800-554-1819

SEEING STARS IS A REGISTERED TRADEMARK OF NANCI BELL.

24   23   22   21   18   19   20   21
ISBN 0-945856-22-9   978-0-945856-22-1

Overview and Directions

Seeing Stars® Decoding Workbooks are supplementary to the *Seeing Stars* program. The goal is to develop *decoding skills* and stimulate symbol imagery as a primary sensory-cognitive function necessary for monitoring, self-correction, and fluency in reading and spelling tasks.

Multisyllables:

Multisyllable processing is an integral part of the Seeing Stars program. Workbook 6, the second of two multisyllable workbooks, provides:

- a review of the basics of multisyllables,
- an introduction, review, and practice with frequently used affixes,
- an introduction to meanings and linquistic origins of common affixes,
- reading and spelling practice with three- and four-syllable words, and
- writing exercises.

Decode, Decode, Decode the Reading List:

Students need to decode, decode, decode—and there are 680 words in each of the first four workbooks, and about 900 words each in workbooks 5 and 6.

- There are twenty words in each Reading List to provide your student with practice decoding both nonwords and real words. Along with decoding, at times use the words to stimulate your student's symbol imagery. For example: *"Read the word. Now cover it…and air-write it. What is the fourth letter you picture?"*
- I included nonwords in the reading lists to stimulate phonetic processing. Since memory and/or oral vocabulary cannot aid his word reading, your student has to accurately decode—guessing won't work.
- If your student spells a word phonetically, accept the phonological representation as possible, but don't leave your student with an inaccurate visual imprint for the word. Show him the real way to spell the word and help him create a mental representation for the meaning: *"The word 'nature' is spelled like this. See it and write it in the air. Here's what you can picture for the meaning of the word 'nature.'"*

The Blank Spelling List:

Use the blank spaces on the Spelling List to have your student spell words appropriate to the phonological and orthographic patterns presented on the page. Do not have him spell the exact same words he just read on the Reading List of that page! Instead, use words from a previous list, make up your own, or use a spelling list from school. Most important, if decoding is your focus, don't have your student spell all ten words. Instead, have him read twenty and spell five. Remember, decode, decode, decode!

Sentence and Paragraph Writing:

This workbook includes opportunities for students to write sentences and short paragraphs. Direct your student to visualize the story starters and then to remember to create images in his own writing. If decoding is the focus of your instruction, have your student complete the story starter exercises in one or two sentences. If he needs more practice writing, you can have him write a longer paragraph on a separate sheet of paper. Note the use of adjectives in most of the story starters—student responses should also include adjectives to describe their imagery.

Group Stimulation:

The workbooks are used for both individual and group practice. Each student should have a book. In small groups or whole classrooms, all students respond to your instruction. Call on a student to read a specific word and keep others involved by signaling agreement or not, as in, *"Buzz, read number three, and say the vowel first. The rest of you, give thumbs up or down."* For spelling, say the word to be spelled, then call on a student to spell it aloud: *"Buzz, tell us how you spelled the word 'slipper.' Thumbs up or down, everyone? Now let's all spell it in the air."*

For paragraph writing, simply take turns and then discuss the concept imagery. Easy!

Affix Overview:

This workbook provides practice at the three- and four-syllable level for common suffixes and Latin prefixes introduced in *Multisyllable Decoding Workbook 5*. New Latin prefixes are also introduced and practiced. The following lists outline the affixes practiced in this workbook.

Common Suffixes Reviewed

ly	dle	er	tive	sion	cial	ious	io
tle	gle	ar	sive	tious	sia	ion	ic
ple	zle	or	ous	cious	ia	gious	ist
ble	cle	ment	ent	tience	ial	gion	ify
fle	ful	less	ence	tient	ian	a	ery
sle	al	ness	ance	cient	ience	age	
kle	ing	ture	tion	tial	ient	ate	

Latin Prefixes Reviewed

pro	con	trans
pre	ex	de
dis	re	
in	com	

Latin Prefixes Introduced

ab	contra	per	tri
ad	inter	post	
bi	multi	sub	
circum	non	super	

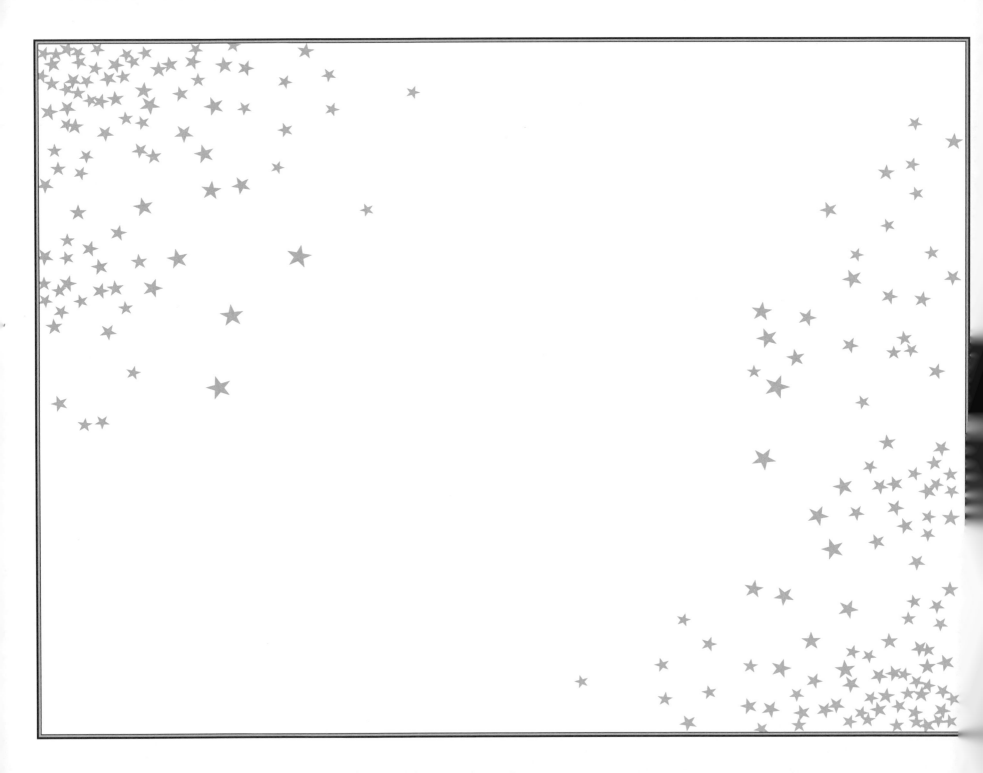

Let's refresh!

Give yourself a plus if you know these!

___ ★ Words have syllables—chunks—you can count.

___ ★ Every syllable has a vowel.

___ ★ Visualize the prefixes and suffixes in words.

___ ★ Use a diagonal line to show the break between syllables.

___ ★ First break words with a PENCIL...then break with your FINGER...then with your EYE.

___ ★ When breaking the word, try to start each syllable with a consonant.

___ ★ An *open* syllable ends in a vowel. The vowel is long, saying its name (go, table).

___ ★ A *closed* syllable ends in a consonant. The vowel is short and doesn't say its name (sit, little).

___ ★ A doubled consonant keeps the vowel short (win to winning, but dine to dining).

___ ★ A schwa is a vowel sound that is neutral because it is unstressed—unaccented—in a syllable.

___ ★ The schwa says /u/.

___ ★ Flex vowel sounds in syllables from long to short to the schwa (/u/).

Date:_____

2 ★ Symbol imagery helps you read and spell accurately!

★ Give yourself a plus if you can picture letters in words.

★ Symbol imagery is the ability to picture the sounds and letters in words.

★ With good symbol imagery, you can RAPIDLY create a mental picture of a word.

★ Symbol imagery is a sensory tool that allows you to monitor and self-correct quickly.

★ You can quickly compare what you read to your own symbol imagery.

★ Symbol imagery helps you

• sound out words,

• memorize sight words for quick and accurate reading in paragraphs, and

• spell phonetically AND accurately (give, not giv; teach, not teech; nature, not nachur).

English can be tricky, but it is not hard when you can hear and visualize letters in words.

Remember, you can do this. You can do anything.

3 Affix refreshment—reading practice

| Give yourself a plus next to each affix you can read quickly. |

 Common Suffixes

Score: ___
54

__ 1. ly	__ 10. zle	__ 19. less	__ 28. tion	__ 37. sia	__ 46. gion
__ 2. tle	__ 11. cle	__ 20. ness	__ 29. sion	__ 38. ia	__ 47. a
__ 3. ple	__ 12. ful	__ 21. ture	__ 30. tious	__ 39. ial	__ 48. age
__ 4. ble	__ 13. al	__ 22. tive	__ 31. cious	__ 40. ian	__ 49. ate
__ 5. fle	__ 14. ing	__ 23. sive	__ 32. tience	__ 41. ience	__ 50. io
__ 6. sle	__ 15. er	__ 24. ous	__ 33. tient	__ 42. ient	__ 51. ic
__ 7. kle	__ 16. ar	__ 25. ent	__ 34. cient	__ 43. ious	__ 52. ist
__ 8. dle	__ 17. or	__ 26. ence	__ 35. tial	__ 44. ion	__ 53. ify
__ 9. gle	__ 18. ment	__ 27. ance	__ 36. cial	__ 45. gious	__ 54. ery

Common Latin Prefixes

Score: ___
10

__ 1. pro	__ 3. dis	__ 5. con	__ 7. re	__ 9. trans
__ 2. pre	__ 4. in	__ 6. ex	__ 8. com	__ 10. de

4 Affix refreshment—spelling practice

Look at the affixes reviewed on page 3. If there are any affixes you didn't read quickly on the first try, write them on the lines below. Then reread each affix, cover it up, picture it, and air-write it.

1._____	14._____	27._____	40._____	53._____
2._____	15._____	28._____	41._____	54._____
3._____	16._____	29._____	42._____	55._____
4._____	17._____	30._____	43._____	56._____
5._____	18._____	31._____	44._____	57._____
6._____	19._____	32._____	45._____	58._____
7._____	20._____	33._____	46._____	59._____
8._____	21._____	34._____	47._____	60._____
9._____	22._____	35._____	48._____	61._____
10._____	23._____	36._____	49._____	62._____
11._____	24._____	37._____	50._____	63._____
12._____	25._____	38._____	51._____	64._____
13._____	26._____	39._____	52._____	

★ *Here are the more difficult suffixes you reviewed. Read each suffix, then cover it up, picture it, and air-write it.*

1. tious	4. tient	7. cial	10. ial	13. ient	16. gious
2. cious	5. cient	8. sia	11. ian	14. ious	17. gion
3. tience	6. tial	9. ia	12. ience	15. ion	

Pencil Break and Read
20

— 1. deceitful
— 2. suddenly
— 3. integral
— 4. imprindle
— 5. agreenal
— 6. frequently
— 7. colossal
— 8. unstable
— 9. powerful
— 10. ancestral

— 11. disciple
— 12. flavorful
— 13. ungainly
— 14. withdrawal
— 15. entitle
— 16. forgetful
— 17. legibly
— 18. pintably
— 19. ramshackle
— 20. proothfully

Spell and Image
10

— 1. _____
— 2. _____
— 3. _____
— 4. _____
— 5. _____
— 6. _____
— 7. _____
— 8. _____
— 9. _____
— 10. _____

Special Practice
Read with **er, ar,** and or say /er/:

1. **trumpeter**
2. **corfendor**
3. **scavenger**
4. **calendar**
5. **circular**
6. **emperor**
7. **accuser**
8. **regular**
9. **commander**
10. **editor!**

Write one sentence using each of the words below.

powerful: _____

_____

suddenly: _____

_____

emperor: _____

_____

NOTE: Flex the vowels in real words.

6 3 syllables with ly, le, ful, and al

Finger Break and Read   20

— 1. utterly
— 2. respectful
— 3. bartinal
— 4. certainly
— 5. playfully
— 6. personal
— 7. marsiffle
— 8. principle
— 9. internal
— 10. plentiful

— 11. awfully
— 12. bedazzled
— 13. totally
— 14. wonderful
— 15. federal
— 16. particle
— 17. gracefully
— 18. negressful
— 19. legally
— 20. candlelit

Spell and Image   10

— 1. ————————
— 2. ————————
— 3. ————————
— 4. ————————
— 5. ————————
— 6. ————————
— 7. ————————
— 8. ————————
— 9. ————————
— 10. ————————

Special Practice
Read with **er, ar,** and **or**:

1. **conductor**
2. **contractor**
3. **vinegar**
4. **consider**
5. **burglar**
6. **protector**
7. **governor**
8. **popular**
9. **slandisher**
10. **senator!**

★ *Choose three words from the reading lists above. Write one sentence using each word on the lines below.*

_____ : _____

_____

_____ : _____

_____

_____ : _____

_____

3 syllables with ly, le, ful, and al

Date:_____

Finger or Eye Break and Read 20

— 1. splendidly
— 2. spectacle
— 3. fanciful
— 4. capable
— 5. dequittal
— 6. skillfully
— 7. merciful
— 8. willingly
— 9. criminal
— 10. general

— 11. honestly
— 12. meaningful
— 13. trustingly
— 14. throanable
— 15. cleverly
— 16. illegal
— 17. principal
— 18. helpfully
— 19. tampuckle
— 20. normally

Spell and Image 10

— 1. _____
— 2. _____
— 3. _____
— 4. _____
— 5. _____
— 6. _____
— 7. _____
— 8. _____
— 9. _____
— 10. _____

Special Practice
Read with **er**, **ar**, and **or**:

1. **jampurger**
2. **discover**
3. **transformer**
4. **predator**
5. **supporter**
6. **similar**
7. **muscular**
8. **vulgarly**
9. **orator**
10. **survivor!**

Read, visualize, and write what might happen next: Timothy was a forgetful young prince in the kingdom of Galvorly. One night he attended a large party with music, dancing, and flavorful foods. Suddenly his father, the king, stopped the music and said, " _____

_____

_____

_____

_____

Date:_____

3 syllables with ment, tive, sive, and ture

Finger Break and Read

20

— 1. tessertive
— 2. inventive
— 3. perceptive
— 4. departure
— 5. detachment
— 6. aggressive
— 7. effective
— 8. signature
— 9. genditure
— 10. responsive

— 11. productive
— 12. imposture
— 13. employment
— 14. intrusive
— 15. supportive
— 16. punishment
— 17. sentiment
— 18. abrasive
— 19. positive
— 20. tablature

Spell and Image

10

— 1. _____
— 2. _____
— 3. _____
— 4. _____
— 5. _____
— 6. _____
— 7. _____
— 8. _____
— 9. _____
— 10. _____

Special Practice
Read with ent, ence, and ance:

1. **observance**
2. **incident**
3. **ambulance**
4. **emergence**
5. **cognizance**
6. **president**
7. **affluence**
8. **commencement**
9. **whistenance**
10. **excellence!**

⭐ *Write one sentence using each of the words below.*

departure: _____

_____

productive: _____

_____

aggressive: _____

_____

9 3 syllables with ment, tive, sive, and ture

Date:_____

Finger or Eye Break and Read $\overline{20}$

— 1. apartment
— 2. objective
— 3. elusive
— 4. importure
— 5. compliment
— 6. protective
— 7. defensive
— 8. indentured
— 9. commenting
— 10. sennitive

— 11. evasive
— 12. armature
— 13. textureless
— 14. intensive
— 15. attractive
— 16. normument
— 17. ornament
— 18. abusive
— 19. unstructured
— 20. government

Spell and Image $\overline{10}$

— 1. _____
— 2. _____
— 3. _____
— 4. _____
— 5. _____
— 6. _____
— 7. _____
— 8. _____
— 9. _____
— 10. _____

Special Practice
Read with **ent**, **ence**, and **ance**:

1. **ignorance**
2. **dintergence**
3. **dependent**
4. **affluence**
5. **opplerance**
6. **detergent**
7. **imbalance**
8. **congruence**
9. **sustenance**
10. **confident!**

Choose three words from the reading lists above. Write one sentence using each word on the lines below.

_____ : _____

_____

_____ : _____

_____

_____ : _____

Date:_____

Eye Break and Read   20

— 1. adjective   — 11. negative
— 2. destructive   — 12. enrapture
— 3. derenture   — 13. nebusive
— 4. passively   — 14. overture
— 5. offensive   — 15. subjective
— 6. instrument   — 16. furniture
— 7. possessive   — 17. pastureland
— 8. creaturely   — 18. sensitive
— 9. enjoyment   — 19. segmented
— 10. combative   — 20. impressive

Spell and Image   10

— 1. _____
— 2. _____
— 3. _____
— 4. _____
— 5. _____
— 6. _____
— 7. _____
— 8. _____
— 9. _____
— 10. _____

Special Practice
Read with ent, ence, and ance:

1. **pertinent**
2. **influence**
3. **attendance**
4. **malcontent**
5. **difference**
6. **elegance**
7. **fammulent**
8. **prominence**
9. **incidence**
10. **performance!**

Read, visualize, and write what might happen next: Karly's dog is very destructive. When she leaves him home alone, he chews on all the furniture. One time, Karly was gone all day, and when she came home, she

_____

_____

_____

_____

_____

11   3 syllable practice

Eye Break and Read   20

— 1. carnival
— 2. messenger
— 3. settlement
— 4. lannular
— 5. importance
— 6. infancy
— 7. eagerly
— 8. defective
— 9. resistance
— 10. equator

— 11. unsaddle
— 12. director
— 13. eventful
— 14. granular
— 15. implement
— 16. explosive
— 17. adderture
— 18. consequent
— 19. inference
— 20. constancy

Spell and Image   10

— 1. _____
— 2. _____
— 3. _____
— 4. _____
— 5. _____
— 6. _____
— 7. _____
— 8. _____
— 9. _____
— 10. _____

Special Practice
Break and read:

1. **imminent**
2. **constructive**
3. **cohesive**
4. **logical**
5. **milligence**
6. **venturer**
7. **bamboozle**
8. **advisor**
9. **perfectly**
10. **masterful!**

Write one sentence using each of the words below.

carnival: _____

_____

explosive: _____

_____

director: _____

_____

12

3 syllables with ti and ci say sh

Date:_____

Pencil or Finger Break and Read $\overline{20}$

— 1. impatience
— 2. potential
— 3. substantial
— 4. Dalmation
— 5. conniption
— 6. prescription
— 7. taxation
— 8. flictioning
— 9. beration
— 10. optional

— 11. provincial
— 12. financial
— 13. commercial
— 14. magician
— 15. clinician
— 16. suspicion
— 17. delicious
— 18. voracious
— 19. efficient
— 20. proficient

Spell and Image $\overline{10}$

— 1. _____
— 2. _____
— 3. _____
— 4. _____
— 5. _____
— 6. _____
— 7. _____
— 8. _____
— 9. _____
— 10. _____

Special Practice
Read with si says /sh/ or /zh/:

1. **cohesion**
2. **compassion**
3. **invasion**
4. **submersion**
5. **seclusion**
6. **explosion**
7. **morosion**
8. **discussion**
9. **obsession**
10. **dimension!**

Choose three words from the reading lists above. Write one sentence using each word on the lines below.

_____ : _____

_____

_____ : _____

_____

_____ : _____

_____

13

3 syllables with ti and ci say sh

Finger or Eye Break and Read
20

— 1. eruption
— 2. specially
— 3. vexation
— 4. patiently
— 5. sequential
— 6. ambitious
— 7. maricious
— 8. smactician
— 9. socially
— 10. musician

— 11. sufficient
— 12. tenacious
— 13. desertion
— 14. fictitious
— 15. impartial
— 16. deficient
— 17. infection
— 18. national
— 19. morsention
— 20. impatient

Spell and Image
10

— 1. _____
— 2. _____
— 3. _____
— 4. _____
— 5. _____
— 6. _____
— 7. _____
— 8. _____
— 9. _____
— 10. _____

Special Practice
Read with si says /sh/ or /zh/:

1. **ambrosia**
2. **erision**
3. **Malaysia**
4. **corrosion**
5. **diffusion**
6. **suspension**
7. **hensional**
8. **compression**
9. **diversion**
10. **comprehension!**

Read, visualize, and write what might happen next: When Samantha was seven years old, she decided to be a magician. She baked a chocolate cake and told her mom she could make it disappear by gobbling it up. The cake looked delicious, but when Samantha took her first bite, _____

_____

_____

_____

_____

14 3 syllables with i says ee

Finger Break and Read —20

- — 1. farbial
- — 2. phobia
- — 3. trickier
- — 4. champion
- — 5. trivial
- — 6. genial
- — 7. median
- — 8. shimmian
- — 9. ruffian
- — 10. radiance
- — 11. variant
- — 12. audience
- — 13. gradient
- — 14. thermient
- — 15. funnier
- — 16. cloudiest
- — 17. media
- — 18. lenience
- — 19. axial
- — 20. ambience

Spell and Image —10

- — 1. _____
- — 2. _____
- — 3. _____
- — 4. _____
- — 5. _____
- — 6. _____
- — 7. _____
- — 8. _____
- — 9. _____
- — 10. _____

Special Practice
Read with ous:

1. **nervousness**
2. **devious**
3. **lintacious**
4. **poisonous**
5. **bramously**
6. **infamous**
7. **callousness**
8. **audacious**
9. **glorious**
10. **momentous!**

⭐ *Write one sentence using each of the words below.*

trickier: _____

_____

audience: _____

_____

champion: _____

_____

15 — 3 syllables with i says ee

Date:_____

Eye Break and Read
20

- 1. mania
- 2. medial
- 3. simian
- 4. deviance
- 5. tedious
- 6. Indian
- 7. jovial
- 8. ambient
- 9. scorpion
- 10. obvious

- 11. copious
- 12. denvient
- 13. menial
- 14. smelliest
- 15. bampion
- 16. hernia
- 17. pranial
- 18. poriance
- 19. salience
- 20. orient

Spell and Image
10

- 1. _____
- 2. _____
- 3. _____
- 4. _____
- 5. _____
- 6. _____
- 7. _____
- 8. _____
- 9. _____
- 10. _____

Special Practice
Read with **ous**:

1. **odorous**
2. **ponderous**
3. **boisterous**
4. **cancerous**
5. **gellious**
6. **odious**
7. **scandalous**
8. **nervously**
9. **callousness**
10. **marvelous!**

Read, visualize, and write what might happen next: The smelliest monster of all lives in a dark corner of the forest. He is a jovial creature despite his stench. One day, two kids were exploring the forest when they discovered

_____

_____

_____

_____

_____

16 ★ 3 syllables with gious, geous, gion, and gen

Finger or Eye Break and Read
_____ 20

— 1. contagious	— 11. subregion
— 2. allergen	— 12. religious
— 3. regional	— 13. lapragious
— 4. outrageous	— 14. litigious
— 5. thregional	— 15. hirstigious
— 6. gorgeously	— 16. hydrogen
— 7. rampageous	— 17. egregious
— 8. contagion	— 18. bedrageous
— 9. shundigious	— 19. religion
— 10. nitrogen	— 20. cedregion

Spell and Image
_____ 10

— 1. _____

— 2. _____

— 3. _____

— 4. _____

— 5. _____

— 6. _____

— 7. _____

— 8. _____

— 9. _____

— 10. _____

★ Special Practice
Read with a at the end:

1. **fibula**

2. **militia**

3. **spadula**

4. **corona**

5. **inertia**

6. **opera**

7. **senatia**

8. **patella**

9. **aurora**

10. **novella!**

★ *Make up a story about catching a contagious disease that makes you grow horns.*

_____

_____

_____

_____

_____

_____

17   3 syllables with age and ate

Finger Break and Read   20

- 1. foliage
- 2. temperate
- 3. vertebrate
- 4. overage
- 5. advantage
- 6. skittimate
- 7. pilgrimage
- 8. bralliage
- 9. corporate
- 10. estimate
- 11. hermitage
- 12. leverage
- 13. passionate
- 14. appendage
- 15. sharnicate
- 16. patronage
- 17. moderate
- 18. gobbitage
- 19. desperate
- 20. literate

Spell and Image   10

- 1. _____
- 2. _____
- 3. _____
- 4. _____
- 5. _____
- 6. _____
- 7. _____
- 8. _____
- 9. _____
- 10. _____

Special Practice
Read with ic, ist, and ify:

1. **classify**
2. **motorist**
3. **petrify**
4. **angelic**
5. **trompify**
6. **activist**
7. **concentric**
8. **finalist**
9. **volcanic**
10. **fantastic!**

Choose three words from the reading lists above. Write one sentence using each word on the lines below.

_____: _____

_____

_____: _____

_____

_____: _____

3 syllable practice...begin 4 syllables

Date: _____

Pencil or Finger Break and Read 20

- ___ 1. inviting
- ___ 2. colorless
- ___ 3. boyishly
- ___ 4. saliva
- ___ 5. exfotion
- ___ 6. component
- ___ 7. connenture
- ___ 8. decency
- ___ 9. occurrence
- ___ 10. partially
- ___ 11. potentially
- ___ 12. fundamental
- ___ 13. impatiently
- ___ 14. emotional
- ___ 15. invermulence
- ___ 16. miniature
- ___ 17. effectively
- ___ 18. amphibious
- ___ 19. controversial
- ___ 20. insufficient

Spell and Image 10

- ___ 1. _____
- ___ 2. _____
- ___ 3. _____
- ___ 4. _____
- ___ 5. _____
- ___ 6. _____
- ___ 7. _____
- ___ 8. _____
- ___ 9. _____
- ___ 10. _____

Special Practice
Read with ic, ist, and ify:

1. **impressionist**
2. **solidify**
3. **nationalist**
4. **prestarlify**
5. **identical**
6. **unspecific**
7. **seculemist**
8. **minimalist**
9. **personify**
10. **linguistical!**

Write one sentence using each of the words below.

miniature: _____

_____

amphibious: _____

_____

saliva: _____

_____

19 4 syllable affix practice

Finger Break and Read
20

— 1. diversify
— 2. pernitially
— 3. fanatical
— 4. affectionate
— 5. desperately
— 6. locomotive
— 7. suburbia
— 8. previously
— 9. hectorial
— 10. obedience

— 11. expatriate
— 12. horticulture
— 13. sufficiency
— 14. primordial
— 15. equestrian
— 16. affirmative
— 17. ingredient
— 18. peculiar
— 19. acclimension
— 20. literature

Spell and Image
10

— 1. _____
— 2. _____
— 3. _____
— 4. _____
— 5. _____
— 6. _____
— 7. _____
— 8. _____
— 9. _____
— 10. _____

Special Practice
Read with **ery** and **ory**:

1. **forgery**
2. **history**
3. **cutlery**
4. **factory**
5. **pernery**
6. **ivory**
7. **mizery**
8. **snobbery**
9. **witchery**
10. **sensory!**

Choose three words from the reading lists above. Write one sentence using each word on the lines below.

_____ : _____

_____

_____ : _____

_____

_____ : _____

20 4 syllable practice

Eye Break and Read
20

— 1. disqualify
— 2. nonconformist
— 3. setteranic
— 4. informative
— 5. agriculture
— 6. efficiency
— 7. congenial
— 8. financially
— 9. custodian
— 10. conglomerate

— 11. expedience
— 12. impervious
— 13. rufagiously
— 14. harmonious
— 15. millenia
— 16. pessimistic
— 17. deliberate
— 18. separately
— 19. temperature
— 20. cumulative

Spell and Image
10

— 1. _____
— 2. _____
— 3. _____
— 4. _____
— 5. _____
— 6. _____
— 7. _____
— 8. _____
— 9. _____
— 10. _____

Special Practice
Read with **ery** and **ory**:

1. **perfunctory**
2. **delivery**
3. **sanzatory**
4. **compulsory**
5. **recovery**
6. **artillery**
7. **allegory**
8. **directory**
9. **effrontery**
10. **entomery!**

Read, visualize, and write what might happen next: The mad scientist poured the colorless liquid into the beaker. Then he added a scoop of special green powder—the last component—to the mixture. Instantly, the mixture started to _____

_____

_____

_____

_____

Date:_____

Latin prefixes and what they mean

Prefixes help you know the meaning of a word. Many common prefixes come from the Latin language. Say, see (visualize), and air-write the following Latin prefixes, and then visualize their meanings.

Latin Prefixes

ab	(away from)	de	(down, not)	per	(through)	super	(above, greater)
ad	(to, toward)	dis	(missing, taken away)	post	(after)	trans	(across)
bi	(two)	ex	(out of)	pre	(before)	tri	(three)
circum	(around)	inter	(between)	pro	(for, forward)		
com	(with, together)	multi	(many)	re	(again, back)		
contra	(against)	non	(not)	sub	(under)		

 Draw a line to match each of the words below to its correct definition.

precaution •   • to speak suddenly or cry out, as in surprise

proactive •   • something done to protect against a future risk

deconstruct •   • done with no pauses or stops in the process

discontent •   • to take apart or break down into pieces

nonstop •   • being without happiness or contentment

exclaim •   • acting to prepare for something to happen

Date:_____

Pencil or Finger Break and Read   20

- — 1. pretender
- — 2. presumption
- — 3. projector
- — 4. precession
- — 5. prevailing
- — 6. proceeding
- — 7. production
- — 8. precancel
- — 9. precaution
- —10. prolation
- — 11. prediction
- — 12. procrastile
- — 13. propulsion
- — 14. pregainful
- — 15. precisely
- — 16. protractor
- — 17. protester
- — 18. preventive
- — 19. prospective
- — 20. pronouncement

Spell and Image   10

- — 1. _____
- — 2. _____
- — 3. _____
- — 4. _____
- — 5. _____
- — 6. _____
- — 7. _____
- — 8. _____
- — 9. _____
- —10. _____

★★ Special Practice ★
Read with 4 syllables:

1. **competitive**
2. **electrician**
3. **colonial**
4. **compassionate**
5. **ultimately**
6. **excusional**
7. **industrious**
8. **legislature**
9. **identify**
10. **sensational!**

★ *Read, visualize, and write what might happen next:* Ernesto works at a jet propulsion lab. He wants to develop a jet plane that can fly into outer space. He takes many precautions when working on the rocket engines, like wearing safety goggles. But one afternoon _____

_____

_____

_____

_____

23 4 syllables with pre and pro

Date:_____

Finger or Eye Break and Read — 20

1. precipitous
2. provisional
3. pretentiously
4. professional
5. pretenturely
6. preconception
7. prozonishment
8. propensity
9. proportional
10. precursory
11. proverbial
12. predicament
13. predictable
14. profanity
15. procrastinate
16. processional
17. predominant
18. probational
19. projectionist
20. precondition

Spell and Image — 10

1. _____
2. _____
3. _____
4. _____
5. _____
6. _____
7. _____
8. _____
9. _____
10. _____

Special Practice
Read with 4 syllables:

1. **preposterous**
2. **familiar**
3. **slopiciousness**
4. **comprehensive**
5. **musculature**
6. **appronical**
7. **integration**
8. **apprehensive**
9. **equivalent**
10. **proficiency!**

Review and visualize the meanings of the following Latin prefixes. Then match each word below to its correct definition.

re (again, back)   post (after)   inter (between)   per (through)   sub (under)   super (above, greater)

remodel •
postmodern •
interstate •
permutate •
substandard •
superman •

• very modern; cutting edge
• not meeting up to what is expected
• to make or build again in a new way
• to change something to a different form
• a person with very great powers
• involving or connecting more than one state

24 ★ 3 syllables with de, dis, non, and ex

Finger Break and Read
₂₀

— 1. deception
— 2. nondescript
— 3. disarray
— 4. execute
— 5. nonfiction
— 6. departure
— 7. exactly
— 8. disembark
— 9. deficient
— 10. nonlimment

— 11. disable
— 12. excitement
— 13. nonstandard
— 14. descendant
— 15. exception
— 16. disjointed
— 17. demolish
— 18. nonprofit
— 19. discretious
— 20. exclusion

Spell and Image
₁₀

— 1. _____
— 2. _____
— 3. _____
— 4. _____
— 5. _____
— 6. _____
— 7. _____
— 8. _____
— 9. _____
— 10. _____

★ Special Practice
Read with 4 syllables:

1. **intensify**
2. **preservative**
3. **prevendibly**
4. **manufacture**
5. **remedial**
6. **legitimate**
7. **promolation**
8. **notorious**
9. **appropriate**
10. **illustrious!**

★ *Read, visualize, and write what might happen next:* The passengers buzzed with excitement as they disembarked the cruise ship. But once they stepped ashore on the tropical island, they _____

_____

_____

_____

| REMEMBER: Flex the open vowels from long to short to the schwa. |

25 4 syllables with de, dis, non, and ex

Date:_____

Finger or Eye Break and Read
20

— 1. degenerate
— 2. nonflammable
— 3. disorient
— 4. demuctible
— 5. exceedingly
— 6. disinterest
— 7. delectable
— 8. nonengortive
— 9. exhibition
— 10. nonconductor

— 11. excavation
— 12. disansibly
— 13. demoralize
— 14. exploration
— 15. deformation
— 16. nonrestrictive
— 17. explotively
— 18. disharmony
— 19. exclamation
— 20. derivative

Spell and Image
10

— 1. _____
— 2. _____
— 3. _____
— 4. _____
— 5. _____
— 6. _____
— 7. _____
— 8. _____
— 9. _____
— 10. _____

Special Practice
Read with 4 syllables:

1. **automotive**
2. **ambidextrous**
3. **proquentific**
4. **contortionist**
5. **nomenclature**
6. **memorial**
7. **delicately**
8. **immaculate**
9. **historian**
10. **magnificent!**

Review and visualize the meanings of the following Latin prefixes. Then match each word below to its correct definition.

ab (away from)   **ad** (to, toward)   **com** (with, together)   **bi** (two)   **tri** (three)   **multi** (many)

abnormal •

adjoining •

compassion •

biweekly •

triangle •

multitask •

• being next to or in contact with something

• a shape having three sides and three corners

• doing more than one thing at a time

• happening once every two weeks

• deep feeling for another's suffering

• weird; far from typical or normal

Date:_____

3 syllables with re, pre, post, and inter

Eye Break and Read

20

— 1. reception
— 2. precursor
— 3. postfrontal
— 4. interact
— 5. receiver
— 6. precocious
— 7. postmaster
— 8. interest
— 9. reflective
— 10. postimate

— 11. presuppose
— 12. postglacial
— 13. intermal
— 14. refurbish
— 15. postponement
— 16. interview
— 17. prevention
— 18. resemblance
— 19. precision
— 20. interject

Spell and Image

10

— 1. _____
— 2. _____
— 3. _____
— 4. _____
— 5. _____
— 6. _____
— 7. _____
— 8. _____
— 9. _____
— 10. _____

Special Practice

Read with de, dis, non, and ex:

1. **nonverbal**
2. **expensive**
3. **disassemble**
4. **deflation**
5. **dependency**
6. **disengage**
7. **nonvittent**
8. **noncommittal**
9. **definitive**
10. **excellent!**

Read, visualize, and write what might happen next: The doorbell rang twice before Darnell opened the door. What he discovered on his front porch caught his interest right away. It was _____

_____

_____

_____

_____

Finger or Eye Break and Read   20

— 1. responsible
— 2. preferable
— 3. postgraduate
— 4. interstellar
— 5. intermission
— 6. prehistoric
— 7. reversible
— 8. redundancy
— 9. presentable
— 10. postrenatience

— 11. preoccupied
— 12. relationship
— 13. interconnect
— 14. preeminent
— 15. rebalancing
— 16. internazzle
— 17. repostable
— 18. replantation
— 19. intermittent
— 20. presentiment

Spell and Image   10

— 1. _____
— 2. _____
— 3. _____
— 4. _____
— 5. _____
— 6. _____
— 7. _____
— 8. _____
— 9. _____
— 10. _____

Special Practice
Read with de, dis, non, and ex:

1. **expectation**
2. **devotion**
3. **discrepancy**
4. **nonexurbance**
5. **disloyal**
6. **nonlethal**
7. **displatiently**
8. **delirious**
9. **nonresistant**
10. **exceptional!**

Write one sentence using each of the words below.

prehistoric: _____

_____

responsible:_____

_____

intermission: _____

_____

28 3 syllables with per, pro, sub, and super

Date:_____

Finger Break and Read   20

— 1. perfidy
— 2. procedure
— 3. subtendrum
— 4. superman
— 5. percussion
— 6. prohibit
— 7. subcentral
— 8. supervise
— 9. perspective
— 10. propenseful

— 11. subconscious
— 12. superscript
— 13. permanence
— 14. protrusion
— 15. subculture
— 16. supersede
— 17. performer
— 18. progressive
— 19. submissive
— 20. superbly

Spell and Image   10

— 1. _____
— 2. _____
— 3. _____
— 4. _____
— 5. _____
— 6. _____
— 7. _____
— 8. _____
— 9. _____
— 10. _____

Special Practice
Read with re, pre, post, and inter:

1. **premeditate**
2. **reprisal**
3. **postampulate**
4. **preconceive**
5. **intervene**
6. **posthumous**
7. **presentiously**
8. **intercept**
9. **postnatal**
10. **refinement!**

Read, visualize, and write what might happen next: The circus performers ran into the tent and the crowd cheered. A woman acrobat climbed a high tower and swung by her legs from a trapeze. Suddenly, one leg slipped off the bar and she _____

_____

_____

_____

_____

4 syllables with per, pro, sub, and super

Finger or Eye Break and Read

$\frac{}{20}$

— 1. peremptory
— 2. sublimation
— 3. perfumery
— 4. percentiently
— 5. profundity
— 6. subuminal
— 7. superstition
— 8. proportionment
— 9. supercharger
— 10. subordinate

— 11. superstatious
— 12. perforated
— 13. superficial
— 14. suborbital
— 15. prohibitive
— 16. prodevian
— 17. suburbanite
— 18. perceptible
— 19. permutation
— 20. supervision

Spell and Image

$\frac{}{10}$

— 1. _____
— 2. _____
— 3. _____
— 4. _____
— 5. _____
— 6. _____
— 7. _____
— 8. _____
— 9. _____
— 10. _____

Special Practice

Read with **re**, **pre**, **post**, and **inter**:

1. **rewarding**
2. **postdated**
3. **previous**
4. **postcarlition**
5. **intercession**
6. **reluctantly**
7. **resurgence**
8. **interaxily**
9. **refinery**
10. **remarkable!**

Choose three words from the reading lists above. Write one sentence using each word on the lines below.

_____: _____

_____

_____: _____

_____

_____: _____

Date:_____

3 syllable with ab, ad, com, and contra

Finger Break and Read
20

- ___ 1. abduction
- ___ 2. adaptive
- ___ 3. combustion
- ___ 4. contraband
- ___ 5. abundant
- ___ 6. addition
- ___ 7. commander
- ___ 8. contravene
- ___ 9. abstraction
- ___ 10. adhesive
- ___ 11. commission
- ___ 12. contradict
- ___ 13. absolute
- ___ 14. adventure
- ___ 15. complation
- ___ 16. contraption
- ___ 17. abnormal
- ___ 18. admittance
- ___ 19. compromise
- ___ 20. contrastive

Spell and Image
10

- ___ 1. _____
- ___ 2. _____
- ___ 3. _____
- ___ 4. _____
- ___ 5. _____
- ___ 6. _____
- ___ 7. _____
- ___ 8. _____
- ___ 9. _____
- ___ 10. _____

Special Practice
Read with per, pro, sub, and super:

1. **permission**
2. **subversively**
3. **superlative**
4. **proponage**
5. **subtitle**
6. **provocative**
7. **supernal**
8. **perforation**
9. **subcommittee**
10. **perfection!**

Write a story and use at least three words from above.

_____

_____

_____

_____

_____

_____

Date:_____

Finger or Eye Break and Read
₂₀

— 1. adolescence
— 2. combination
— 3. absorbency
— 4. contraception
— 5. abdulify
— 6. composition
— 7. adoration
— 8. aberration
— 9. compilation
— 10. admenageous

— 11. contravention
— 12. contrastively
— 13. adversary
— 14. contraspected
— 15. absolution
— 16. commiserate
— 17. complicity
— 18. adorable
— 19. absurdity
— 20. compensation

Spell and Image
₁₀

— 1. _____
— 2. _____
— 3. _____
— 4. _____
— 5. _____
— 6. _____
— 7. _____
— 8. _____
— 9. _____
— 10. _____

Special Practice
Read with per, pro, sub, and super:

1. **subdivide**
2. **prosoliage**
3. **superpower**
4. **subtraction**
5. **pernicious**
6. **superscribe**
7. **professor**
8. **progressional**
9. **subliminal**
10. **perfectionist!**

Write one sentence using each of the words below.

adversary: _____

_____

professor: _____

_____

superpower: _____

_____

32 3 syllables with bi, tri, and multi

Eye Break and Read
_20_

___ 1. multifold

___ 2. bimotored

___ 3. triangle

___ 4. trimester

___ 5. bisecting

___ 6. multiplex

___ 7. bicolor

___ 8. trivia

___ 9. binisfy

___ 10. trifocals

___ 11. tripedal

___ 12. bifurcate

___ 13. multiphase

___ 14. bilingual

___ 15. trinity

___ 16. multistage

___ 17. trinolate

___ 18. miltiple

___ 19. triplicate

___ 20. bipolar

Spell and Image
_10_

___ 1. _____

___ 2. _____

___ 3. _____

___ 4. _____

___ 5. _____

___ 6. _____

___ 7. _____

___ 8. _____

___ 9. _____

___ 10. _____

Special Practice
Read with ab, ad, com, and contra:

1. **abrasion**

2. **adjacent**

3. **compounded**

4. **contramation**

5. **contractible**

6. **complexity**

7. **abbrensiveness**

8. **administer**

9. **commoditive**

10. **compelling!**

Choose three words from the reading lists above. Write one sentence using each word on the lines below.

_____: _____

_____

_____: _____

_____

_____: _____

_____

Date:_____

Finger or Eye Break and Read
20

— 1. bilateral
— 2. triangular
— 3. tricuspidal
— 4. multisection
— 5. bicarbonate
— 6. trinomial
— 7. multicolored
— 8. biaxial
— 9. binocular
— 10. triceratops

— 11. multilingual
— 12. biannual
— 13. trivially
— 14. tridolorous
— 15. multiplier
— 16. triplicating
— 17. tridentible
— 18. multilevel
— 19. tribulation
— 20. multiratience

Spell and Image
10

— 1. _____
— 2. _____
— 3. _____
— 4. _____
— 5. _____
— 6. _____
— 7. _____
— 8. _____
— 9. _____
— 10. _____

Special Practice
Read with ab, ad, com, and contra:

1. **adjoining**
2. **committee**
3. **absorption**
4. **commendation**
5. **adjustment**
6. **complement**
7. **abusively**
8. **admirable**
9. **contralamen**
10. **commendable!**

★ *Read, visualize, and write what might happen next:* **Maria awoke in the middle of the night to a loud roar coming from her backyard. When she looked out her window, she saw a multicolored triceratops running across the lawn, straight at her back door! She** _____

_____

_____

_____

Date:_____

3-4 syllables with Latin prefixes

Eye Break and Read
20

— 1. superstitious
— 2. multiform
— 3. reprostripted
— 4. compromising
— 5. internestor
— 6. delightful
— 7. contradiction
— 8. comfortable
— 9. bifunctional
— 10. postdoctoral

— 11. nonhuman
— 12. perspiration
— 13. interjector
— 14. abstraction
— 15. trimonthly
— 16. disadvantange
— 17. extension
— 18. prevesionate
— 19. subkingdom
— 20. productiveness

Spell and Image
10

— 1. _____
— 2. _____
— 3. _____
— 4. _____
— 5. _____
— 6. _____
— 7. _____
— 8. _____
— 9. _____
— 10. _____

Special Practice
Read with **circum** and **trans**:

1. **transportation**
2. **circumference**
3. **circumstantial**
4. **transitional**
5. **circumlution**
6. **transcendental**
7. **circumvention**
8. **transitory**
9. **circumrotate**
10. **transfiguring!**

Write a story and use at least three words from above.

_____

_____

_____

_____

_____

3-4 syllables with Latin prefixes

Date:_____

Eye Break and Read
20

— 1. proportional
— 2. transmoblitive
— 3. disinterment
— 4. circumscription
— 5. regenerate
— 6. trilingual
— 7. persecution
— 8. multiplying
— 9. competition
— 10. disenchant

— 11. contrasting
— 12. antelicious
— 13. nondestructive
— 14. biyearly
— 15. superfluous
— 16. advantageous
— 17. premonition
— 18. demented
— 19. explanation
— 20. substantially

Spell and Image
10

— 1. _____
— 2. _____
— 3. _____
— 4. _____
— 5. _____
— 6. _____
— 7. _____
— 8. _____
— 9. _____
— 10. _____

Special Practice
Read with 4 syllables:

1. **deciduous**
2. **reciprocal**
3. **protestation**
4. **superhuman**
5. **nondistinctive**
6. **perennial**
7. **excitable**
8. **subsequently**
9. **preponderance**
10. **exemplary!**

Read, visualize, and write what might happen next: The number of bats in Kim's neighborhood was multiplying rapidly. There were substantially more flitting around the trees and houses than just a few days before. One day Kim and her little sister discovered the explanation: _____

_____

_____

_____

_____

Notes